ISBN: 9781314929102

Published by:
HardPress Publishing
8345 NW 66TH ST #2561
MIAMI FL 33166-2626

Email: info@hardpress.net
Web: http://www.hardpress.net

Division

Section

The
Hidden
Years at
Nazareth

The Hidden
Years at Nazareth

By
Rev. G. Campbell Morgan

Pastor of New Court Congregational Church
Tollington Park, London

Author of
Discipieship

New York   Chicago   Toronto
Fleming H. Revell Company
Publishers of Evangelical Literature

"Thou art My beloved Son, in whom
I am well pleased."—Mark i. 11.

"Is not this the carpenter?"
Mark vi. 3.

The Hidden Years
at Nazareth

❧

THE soul's first vision of Jesus is of Him as the Saviour. When we so know Him, He becomes to us the exemplar, leaving us an example, that we should follow in His steps. He is more than an example in any ordinary acceptation of that term, for He not only reveals to us the pattern of our lives, but He also brings the power by which we

may grow up into Him in all
things, and so reproduce in
actual living the perfect and
wondrous pattern that He
shows. But we must clearly
understand that we never get
back into the life of Jesus save
by the way of His death. His
death is evermore the gate of
life to man — not only a gate
to the eternal life that stretches
beyond this place and time of
conflict, but the gate into the
eternal life which we live to-
day, if we are living in direct
and positive communion with
Himself. Having known Him
as the Saviour, and having
found our way into the realm

8

of life at the cross, then He becomes our example, and all that He is in the revelation of the fourfold gospel marks His intention for His people.

Now, beloved, let us seek to learn the purpose of Christ for us in one particular department of life.

It is not given to every man or woman to serve God in public places; the great majority must live their lives outside any prominent sphere, and as part of a very small circle of relatives and acquaintances. Men will not hear even the names of the great mass of the people who are living their life throughout the world to-day. I want to know what there is in the life of Jesus that helps such persons. We are accustomed to think of Him as one in a public ministry, as the man of the market-place and the crowd, the teacher who "spake as never man spake," the healer whose touch brought life and blessing to hundreds, the man who rebuked sin in high places and spoke words of infinitely sweet pity and kindness to the child and the young disciple; but the greater part of His life was not lived in those places where we have grown most familiar with Him, but in quiet seclusion, where the great crowd of men and women will always live in this world. Yet how little we know concerning that period! how meager is the biblical information! I do not say it is not enough; I believe it is enough; but in the mere matter of words, how small it is! I have the story of His birth, and then I lose sight of Him for twelve years. Then I see Him again, going out to His Jewish confirmation, becoming the son of the law in that Jewish congregation, asking questions of the doctors,

11

and answering theirs. Ah, it
is a wonderful glimpse, a glit-
tering flash, and then I lose
Him again for eighteen long
years, at the end of which time
He comes to be baptized of
John in Jordan, and begins His
public ministry, and I see a
few rapid pictures of miracles
and tears and love and sym-
pathy, and He is gone! If
you will write, in the manner
in which the lives of the men
of to-day are written, the story
of the daily life of Jesus, how
diminutive and meager it is!

What of those eighteen
years? Where was He? What
was He doing? As one whom

He has ordained to preach His gospel in this public ministry, I am intensely interested in the way He spoke to men and acted among men in His public years; but the majority will feel that they would be better served by a revelation of how He acted amid the commonplace surroundings of everyday life.

Let us, then, try and see Him in those eighteen hidden years. The two verses that I have read are the only two that give us any definite or detailed account of what Jesus was doing from the time He was twelve until He was about thirty. Take the two statements and fix them on your minds for a moment: "Thou art My beloved Son, in whom I am well pleased." "Is not this the carpenter?" These two passages supply the story of the eighteen years. Jesus was a carpenter pleasing God. But is it fair to put them together like that? I think you will see that it is. Upon what occasion did that divine voice speak? On the occasion of the baptism. Jesus had left behind all the doings of those long and weary years, and He was just at the dividing-line between private and public life. He was leaving behind Him the unknown years, and coming out into the fierce light that beats ever upon a public teacher. And there, at the parting of the ways, God lit up all the years that had gone with the sweet words of approval, "Thou art My beloved Son, in whom I am well pleased." It could not have been a pronouncement upon the temptation of the wilderness; that was as yet an untried pathway. It could not have been a declaration of the divine pleasure with Gethsemane's garden and Calvary's cross; they were still to be

15

reached. No; it must have
been a reference to the past, so
that, whatever else I know, or
do not know, about the hidden years of the life of Jesus,
this one thing is certain, that
through them all He pleased
God; for God put His seal
upon them when they were
closing behind Him and the
new years were opening before Him, saying: "I am well
pleased." You remember
how, after that pronouncement, He went to the wilderness and was tempted, and
after that temptation He went
to Galilee, in the power of the
Spirit, and began His public

ministry; and you find Him going at the early part thereof down to Nazareth, the place where He has been brought up. It was a small town, a kind of hamlet on the hillside, of perhaps three thousand inhabitants.

This young man comes back to His boyhood's home, and every one knows Him. He goes to the synagogue, as was His custom, on the Sabbath day, and reads out of the book, and then He talks to the assembled people; and they look at Him, and listen, wonder the while being depicted on their faces. Cannot you

see the picture?—that little
synagogue, the old Jewish
people, the keen faces looking
at the speaker, and then turn-
ing to each other, saying:
" Whence hath this man these
things? We know Him per-
fectly well; He is the carpenter." Yes; they know Him.
They have watched Him toil-
ing day after day, month
after month, in the work-
shop, bending over the bench
with the tools of His craft in
His hand. They cannot ac-
count for Him as a teacher
because they did not account
for Him as a toiler.

Mark, then, what these people said about Him. Other men made the blunder of saying He was the son of the carpenter; but these men, by a sudden flash, light up for us the eighteen years by saying, "Is not this the carpenter?" I have now two facts concerning this period. I have the testimony of the men who knew Him best, and the testimony of God, who knew Him better than they did. Let us first take the human declaration, "Is not this the carpenter?" and hold it in the light of the divine, "In whom I am well pleased"; and then let us take the divine revelation, "Thou art My beloved Son," and hold it in the light of the human, "Is not this the carpenter?"

I do not want to hide the majesty of this sweet word the "carpenter" by any multiplication of words of mine. If any of you paint pictures, have you not sometimes been annoyed at the way in which men have framed them? You invite your friends' attention to a work of art, and they exclaim, "What a lovely frame!" and do not seem to see the picture. We sometimes frame the picture of God's words in like manner.

Let us express ourselves so that the picture is seen and not the frame. "Is not this the carpenter?" For the greater part, then, of the life of Jesus, He worked with His own hands for His own living. That brings the Son of God, in living, pulsating life, close to every man who works. There is a beautiful tradition, that Joseph, His reputed father, died while Jesus was yet a child, and so He worked not merely to earn His own living, but to keep the little home together in Nazareth, and Mary and the younger members of the family de-

pended upon His toil. That
is a beautiful tradition. It
may be true, but I do not press
it. But I do press this upon
you above everything else,
that He worked for His living. Oh that we could get
all the strength and comfort
which this fact is calculated to
afford! Business men, you
who have been at work all
the week and have been har-
assed by daily labors and are
weary and tired and seeking
for new inspiration, this
Jesus, whose name has be-
come a name of sweetness
and love, was not a king
upon a throne, He was not

for the greater part of His life a teacher with the thrill and excitement of public life to buoy Him up. No; the long years ran on and He was doing what some of you speak of as " the daily round, the common task." The man Jesus rose at daybreak, and, picking up His tools, made yokes and tables in order that He might have something to eat, and that, not for a brief period, but for eighteen years. He was an apprentice boy, a young man improving His craft, a master in His little shop with the shavings round Him and the tools about Him.

23

That is the human picture. But that human picture becomes supremely precious to me as the light of the divine falls upon it. The eighteen years are over, the tools are laid aside, His feet will no more make music as He walks among the rustling shavings. God says, "I am pleased." It may have meant that God was pleased with Jesus because in those years He lived in the realm of the spiritual rather than the material. I believe it did mean that, but I am not going to dwell upon it. It may have meant that He was careful to think of, and pray for, and teach the younger members of His household, or that He was regular in His attendance upon the services of the synagogue. I think it did mean that, because I read, " He went to the synagogue, as was His custom, on the Sabbath day." But I want to know what God meant about the shop, and I am going to suggest to you two things. In the first place,—and you will forgive this way of putting it, because I want the truth of it to abide upon your hearts, and if the phrasing be not elegant I want it to be forceful,—it

25

meant that Jesus had never
done in that carpenter's shop
a piece of work such as we
speak of in the closing years
of the nineteenth century as
being "shoddy work." "I
am pleased." God could not
have been pleased with car-
pentry that was scamped any
more than with blasphemous
praise. "I am pleased," and
every bit of work has on it
the light of divine truth.
When Jesus sent out from
that carpenter's shop yokes
that the farmers would use,
they were so fashioned and
finished that they would gall
no ox. "Take My yoke

upon you " gathers force and
strength as an illustration
from the fidelity of the carpenter's shop. When Jesus
said, " Take My yoke," it
was because He knew that it
would not gall, it would be
finished and perfect. Sometimes we have overshadowed
the carpenter's shop with
Calvary's cross. We have no
right to do it. We have
come to forget the fidelity of
the Son of God in the little
details of life as we have
gazed upon His magnificent
triumphs in the places of passion and conflict. In the
second place, the divine ap-

27

proval meant that the influence of the life had been pure and bright and good. You all know the effect of influence. What sort of influence has He exerted? Pure and strong! I have sat sometimes in meditative mood, and thought of my beloved Lord, and tried to carry myself back, with all the interests that are nearest to my heart, into that land and that time when He was on earth, and I have thought, if I could just have taken my boy and apprenticed him to that carpenter, what a blessed thing it would have been. I don't think Jesus would have given him the One Hundred and Nineteenth Psalm to learn before he came to work in the morning, or have been talking to him forevermore about heaven and getting ready for it, and hell and shunning it. But he would have lived a bright, strong, glad life before Him, for no life ever touched the life of the Son of God but was the brighter and purer and stronger for the contact; and so, when the years of the carpenter's shop are over, God sets His seal of approval upon them, first, because the work has been well

done; and, secondly, because
the influence of the life has
been true and right and noble.

Who is this coming up out
of the waters of baptism,
upon whom the dove hovers
and settles, and concerning
whom heaven's voice is heard
to speak? God marks Him
out here from all His fellow-
men. "Thou art My beloved
Son." Not "Thou art a son,
a child of Mine," but "My
Son." And, to the Hebrew
mind, that links Him with all
the prophecies of the past.
He is the anointed of God.
He is the one personage who
is charged with the great mis-

sion of restoring the kingdom of God. God marks Him in that great word as His appointed Messiah, as Shiloh, as the Daysman from on high, as the Dayspring; all the wondrous words of past prophecy are settled upon Him, and God marks Him as the anointed One for the carrying out of the great scheme of redemption for the human race. And now He is standing on the banks of the Jordan, and we look upon Him for the first time with amazement and astonishment, and wonder, if this be the beloved Son of God, what has He been

31

doing, where has He been in the years preceding this public manifestation? Come back again to the question, "Is not this the carpenter?" and the wonder is presented in a new vision, from a new standpoint, from another side. The Son of God, charged with the greatest commission that any being in heaven or earth has ever had to bear, was for eighteen years at work in a carpenter's shop. Now, we hardly see the wonder of this thing until we look more closely at it. I may be speaking to some young man upon whose heart is lying the burden of India, the need of China; he is travailing in spirit, even in this favored land, for the dark masses of Africa; he is touched with the sacrificial passion of the Son of God to go and save somebody, and yet God has shut him up here at home. He has to live and care for a sick one. He can't go. The fire is there, but the door is not open. The passion for men consumes him, but God shuts him out from service. Now, it is only those who know something of what that experience is who can understand the strange marvel of

the Son of God, commissioned
to do the work that precedes
your passion, the infinitely
greater work, holding in its
grasp and love all the enter-
prises for the uplifting of
man. And yet with that passion upon Him, with the
cross ever before Him and
His ultimate triumph in front,
every morning He goes to
the carpenter's shop, every
day He does work, every
night goes home to rest. I
tell you it is a mystery of
mysteries to us restless spirits.
What does it mean? How is
it that He, the beloved of
God, the anointed of God,

34

can be—there is no irreverence in saying it—content? Now, the answer is here. Jesus lived in the power of the truth, which we are so slow to learn, that there is something infinitely better than doing a great thing for God, and the infinitely better thing is to be where God wants us to be, to do what God wants us to do, and to have no will apart from His—to be able to say:

I worship Thee, sweet will of God,
And all Thy ways adore!
And every day I live, I seem
To love Thee more and more.

Jesus understood that. The carpenter's shop was the will

of God for Him, and therefore
He abode in that shop and
did the work incidental to it.
Now, pray do not misunder-
stand me. From the illustration I used a moment ago,
you may come to think that I
intend to say Jesus did it as a
duty, while He longed for the
cross. Nothing of the kind.
"I delight to do Thy will,
O my God." Go and ask
Him, talk with Him reverently
across the distance of nine-
teen hundred years. "O
Nazarene, where wouldst
Thou rather be to-day, here
among this work, or among
the crowd, healing and teach-

36

ing, and preaching to them ? " and the answer would be, " God's will for Me is in the carpenter's shop, and therefore that is the place of My joy." But I am going to ask you to press this question a little further. Was this a capricious matter, this will of God for Jesus? Does it not look hard and arbitrary that God should have put that saintly soul to such common labor? Why not have let Him face the conflict and get the victory, and hie Him back to heaven? There was a deep necessity in the whole arrangement. Let me put it

superlatively, and say, Calvary's cross would have been
nothing but the tragic ending
of a mistaken life, if it had
not been for the carpenter's
shop! In that carpenter's
shop He fought my battles.
My hardest fight is never
fought when there is a crowd
to applaud or oppose, but
when I am alone. Now, that
was what Jesus was doing for
eighteen years. There was
no crowd to sing "Hosanna";
no other crowd to cry "Cru-
cify Him"; but alone He did
His work and faced all the
subtle forms of temptation
that beset humankind, and

one by one He put His con-
quering foot upon the neck of
them, until the last was baf-
fled and beaten, and His ene-
mies were palsied by the
strong stroke of His pure
right arm. That is what He
was doing. There was ne-
cessity for it, and because of
Nazareth's shop there came
Gethsemane's garden and Calvary's cross, and so, abiding
in the will of God, by victory
upon victory, He won His
final triumph, and so opened
the kingdom of heaven to all
believers.

Now, beloved, from this
study what are we to learn?

I can only write off for you,
very briefly, one or two lessons, and the first is a relative
lesson. I never come back
to this story of the early
years of Christ, and read what
these men of Nazareth said
about Him, without learning
how dangerous a thing it is
to pronounce my little sen-
tence upon any single human
life. O men of Nazareth,
down in that carpenter's shop
that you pass and repass,
where you sometimes pause
and look in and see Him at
His work, there is the One
who spoke and it was done,
who put His compass upon

the deep, who fashioned all things by the word of His power, and you have never seen Him and never known Him, and your estimate of Him is that He is one of you —only a carpenter.   Job's judges and Christ's critics are on a level, and they are on a level with every one of us who tries to pass his sen- tences upon his fellow-men. If people ask you for your ex- planation of the mysterious circumstances of a brother man, tell them it is a mystery of God; for the moment you suggest that there is some- thing wrong somewhere you

may be getting into the re-
gion of blasphemy. Perhaps
that man has been broken on
the wheel by the Potter for a
remaking. "If the Potter
break it upon the wheel, He
shall remake it"; and God's
fairest, highest place of service in the land that lies beyond will be filled by the men
and women who have been
broken upon the wheel on
earth. Do not let us forget
that, and if we cannot understand what God is doing with
that woman whose heart is
crushed and broken with
overwhelming sorrow, let us
be reverently silent, lest we

help the men who drive the nails, and break the Lord's own heart.

But I gather not only this relative lesson; there are personal lessons. The first is this: the phrase "common task" should be struck out of every life. Jesus taught us that all toil is holy if the toiler be holy. Not for the sake of controversy, but as a protest against the misconception of human life, I tell you that no man has any right, simply because he preaches or performs certain functions, to speak of himself as a man in "holy orders." The man who goes

out to work to-morrow morning with his bag on his back
and his tools in it, if he be a
holy man, has claims to that
distinction; and if that man go
down into the carpenter's
shop and saw a piece of tim-
ber, the saw is a vessel of the
sanctuary of God, if the man
is a priest who uses it. All
service is sacred service. I
want you to carry this
thought of the working Christ
into all the days of the coming week, behind the counter
and in the office, and, beloved
sisters, if I may say so, in the
home. Remember that
George Herbert had caught

the very spirit of this lovely thought when he sang of the possibility of sweeping a room and "making that and the action fine." Oh, if we could but get the Christian church, to say nothing of the outside world, free from the stupid and false ideas that this kind of work is honorable, and that is not, what a long way we should be on the road to the millennium! If every business man wrote his letters as though Jesus would have to look over them, what lovely letters we should have! I do not know that they would have tracts in them, —

that is not my point, — but they would be true, robust, honest letters. O you business men, won't you do your business for Christ, realizing that the work you do may be as sacred as my work? Sisters, won't you take the home and make it a holy place for the shining of the Shechinah? If Christ lived the larger part of His life working, then our work is smitten through and through and lit with a new beauty, and we write over it, "Part of God's work for uplifting man."

I learn this lesson also, that no man is fit for the great

places of service who has not
fitted himself by fidelity in
obscurity. You want, you
tell me, to preach the gospel
in China. Are you living it at
home? God does not want
men or women to preach His
gospel anywhere who have
not made it shine in their
own homes. I do not ask,
" Can you do the great work
that hangs upon your hearts? "
but, " Are you doing the pres-
ent work faithfully? " Are
you an Endeavorer, do you
belong to the missionary so-
ciety, that branch or this
branch of the church, and are
you so anxious to get to the

meetings that you rob your master of even five minutes of his time? Christ doesn't count the service, but the five minutes you have stolen. What we want is to feel that if we are to do a big thing in the public service, we must be through and through true in the small things of life. The carpenter's shop made Calvary not a battle-field merely, but a day of triumph that lit heaven and earth with hope; and if you and I would triumph when our Calvary comes, we must triumph in the little things of the common hours.

Date Due

ImTheStory.com

Personalized Classic Books in many genre's

Unique gift for kids, partners, friends, colleagues

Customize:

- Character Names
- Upload your own front/back cover images (optional)
- Inscribe a personal message/dedication on the

  inside page (optional)

Customize many titles Including
- Alice in Wonderland
- Romeo and Juliet
- The Wizard of Oz
- A Christmas Carol
- Dracula
- Dr. Jekyll & Mr. Hyde
- And more...